Who Told You to Be God?

Poems

Marial Awendit

Mwanaka Media and Publishing Pvt Ltd,

Chitungwiza, Zimbabwe

*

Creativity, Wisdom, and Beauty

Publisher: *Mmap*
Mwanaka Media and Publishing Pvt Ltd
24 Svosve Road, Zengeza 1
Chitungwiza, Zimbabwe
mwanaka@yahoo.com
mwanaka13@gmail.com
https://www.mmapublishing.org
www.africanbookscollective.com/publishers/mwanaka-media-and-publishing
https://facebook.com/MwanakaMediaAndPublishing/

Distributed in and outside N. America by African Books Collective
orders@africanbookscollective.com
www.africanbookscollective.com

ISBN: 978-1-77933-138-0
EAN: 9781779331380

© Marial Awendit 2024

All rights reserved.
No part of this book may be reproduced or transmitted in any form or by any means, mechanical or electronic, including photocopying and recording, or be stored in any information storage or retrieval system, without written permission from the publisher

DISCLAIMER
All views expressed in this publication are those of the author and do not necessarily reflect the views of *Mmap*.

Contents:
Prelude
The Pages
5 Self-portraits as a Child in Gaza
The Summit
Rwanda
A Lion
The Men in Suits and Ties
This May be Why I Keep Going for Vacation
Failing Sadness by the River
This is Not a Diss Song
A Leaf is Green
Come See Mawut
drowning a bone
Why All this Talk of Robots
The Squirrel
What I Told the Press
The Bougainvillea
I Also Said Nothing against that Grasshopper
Cradle Crave
Dead Trees
Turbulence
The Anthill
Bad Animals
So When is the Apocalypse
Golden Ladder
Glass Plate
I May not Apply for a Demigod
hail the broken hammer
before levitation
Debris
stories
A Crucible

Dear Crown
Small Mirrors before Mountains
But Your Shadow Drowns a Flea
I Wrote a Poem
Is this the Lake
A Rap Encore for Hunger
A Likely Crime in a Rhyme
The Song of Beams
These Songs
There is Something You Seek
Because You are Just a Poet
Mekanika
The Nile's Burdens
Other Mirrors
A Troubadour's Trouble
Who Told You to Be God?
The Guest
Raining Hope
the tulip
You Could Have Ceased an Entire Holocaust
dappled
The Churchyard Song
The Turtle
The Red Tulips
The Game
War Republic
Golden Eagle
Affidavit
This Says It Is Love
A Lament for a Flower
Lumiére
Jasmine
But Please, Bless Us

Cinematography
Ode for a Post-war Period
To Fruit One's Sight
In My Room
The Deity of Switches
This Place
Camera
Dark Doors
Marshall Islands
The Script

Prelude

This collection contains poems of resistance to tyranny and human cruelty. Most suffering arises from human cruelty, in comparison to wild animals and natural disasters. This collection asserts the value of people and nature against the adversaries such as greed, malevolent complicity, religious and racial bigotry. The triumph of love is what this collection expounds and puts afore.

The second category of poems explores self-discovery and love.

The Pages

Flip the pages:

A bomb falls on the verse
Where Gaza lays.
The fire spreads like a flood
Across the page, erasing
The entire verse,
Setting the whole book ablaze.

Read the verse:

Let the children come to me.
When will verses rise from the pages,
Turn into shrapnel & grenades,
To tear curtains off
The smiles of children?

The forecast blares: bombs,
Children, women,
& shattered walls!

You cannot close the book;
It is no longer here:

The Hamas sleep deep
In the throats of little children.
Perhaps, those children
 Did not go with the Hamas,
To shoot partygoers in Israel.

5 Self-portraits as a Child in Gaza

1

We heard of war from our mothers
Before war arrived,
Tore down walls,
& broke God's china.

2

We cannot find the chalice.
We cannot return to build
The city because the city
Is still getting un-built.

3

They have not yet built a wall
Against dreams,
Against prayers,
Against the news...

My doll and I believe in the Messiah.
Still, we both ran from the airstrikes.

4

We do not live in the sandcastles
We built,
Just as we do not live in Gaza.
The rains come to find us
Braiding our songs.

5

Perhaps, that was not Christ,
Behind the bomb launcher,
Calling for rain upon the land:
'There goes your redemption,
Tearing into a hospital.

The Summit

Because war lacks enough raindrops,
There is need for something else,
To water the rosemary.

Because war may not be a good musician,
We should try guitars, drums, & flutes.
Someone here has a cymbal.

Because war cannot wet the beaches,
Let's go somewhere far from
The tranquility of idle bombs.

Because we prefer a vacation,
Let us leave war in the wild, alone.
Let us see what it can achieve by itself.

Rwanda

A flower sprouts
Out of red paint,
Rinses its petals in rain:
You cannot colour me forever.

Kagame atop the hills blows his horn.
The echoes melt the machetes
& the barricades
Men built with the blades
Of their hurts,
Then he bid national dreams
Green all in the belly of Kigali.

A Lion

Four men in red-chequered blankets
Knotted at their shoulders,
Run among thorny shrubs,
In a place not faraway
From the Maasai Mara.
They lurk with spears and clubs.

A lion, its head in the ribcage
Of a wildebeest, notices them
& runs into a nearby bush.
They remove their knives from their waists
& start talking about one of the four lions
They had killed,
The one that left a scar
On their leader's shoulder.

The Men in Suits and Ties

They came to us like one commercial
For a brand of cigarette:
'Vanilla-flavoured and filtered'
And on its pack it was written:
Excessive smoking is risky!

This May be Why I Keep Going for Vacation,

You tell me to sit at the other side
Of the plywood while you drill holes
Into it with a chainsaw, beloved.
The noise litters with sawdust
The discothèque of my poem.

Failing Sadness by the River

Here, before my tamed smile fades
Before miniature tidings of bliss slide,
Somewhere a man my grades
Grits his teeth in feverish pain;
Fits of pain no actor can exactly train.

I peruse beyond the soaked dark lees
Of this river, while I roast catfishes with grass leaves
And pieces of wood, bits of clay rough on my bare feet.
I clear around the fire lest I set black
 The brown grass hiding my quiet back.
From here, my eyes read water thick and blue-black,
Smoothing and kneading the riverbed's black back,
And how could it sink down a throat,
So in it my rising thirst can float?
Though somewhere in the Sahara of lavish lack
A cupped hand full of it is worth a brag.

December's sun heats my left cheek so it appears greasy,
While by my right cheek, smoke clouds spin a zephyr.

This is Not a Diss Song

All the lies welded on you,
Ariop, accolade-winning lies.
That when you came home one afternoon
And your mother had nothing in your bowl,
You slapped dead an ant.
A miserable lie.
You only struck hard
Sleeping dog, and watched it stir barks
Into the crowd of fan palm trees,
Behind the house, fury red-hot on your face.
That when you are wild-dog hungry,
Everything takes the form of food;
The yellow sun melts into margarine;
Stone turns into bread; dirty water looks like milk;
Rainwater is God's leftover juice.
You only said the white cloud could be
God's butter.
That you were the last in your class.
The teachers did not set what you know.

All the lies welded on you, Ariop!

A Leaf is Green

I'm not looking at everything,
But which do I find easier,
To say a leaf is green
Or a person is pleasant?
What sadness did I bring
To the green acacia trees by the Nile?
What more peace do I bring
To the calves frolicking in the African savannah?

I just begin my song & fold its ends.
I do not hear a grumble.

Come See, Mawut

i

"Giant transformers,
Upon a hill in town,
Are uprooting buildings.
They growl
Like shattered thunders.
The whole town cannot go on
                    A sabbatical.
Come see, Mawut" you say.

… But I am in   the shower
Soaping my hair.

ii

"A brown cow on a truck
En route to the auction center,
Ploughed under a bypass
& got decapitated.
Now, that bleeding head is trapped
Between concrete & a rail.
Would you come see, Mawut?" you say.

…but little Beny
Claws in his birth water,
His umbilical cord not even cut.
It might be his first day in the building
But he shrieks like an alarm.

iii

"Dandruff itches,
Breaking hair rattles
Like threads of polythene.
Black lice made hives
In my head.
Cross the Red Sea.
Come, scratch, Mawut" you say.

…but steaming   spaghetti
Worms whine on my plate
Like injured snakes
& I have not eaten for decade now.

iv

"Mawut, Neil Armstrong shipped back

With him biscuits from the moon.

& grey lunar stones.

The townspeople are gathered.

Come, dance a jig" you say.

…but then a fish's bone

Got stuck down my throat.

I feel one more bone

To my skeleton.

…i said a razorblade

Down

My

Throat.

drowning a bone

do not weld your sight

for long

to the orchestra of wailing

                women.

after we laid him

down on the fractured clay,

we waited for the buzzards

to tear off the meat;

to unearth the white core.

waited a little for Thunder to speak,

but we heard the birds

chirp in the thorn trees.

sometimes,

He is too wise for words,

so we signaled the white ants

to wipe grease & black blood

off the bones,

then   sprinkled

into the sun-glazed river

the dry bones.

the splashes cracked

the same tone

as for woods or pebbles.

Why All this Talk of Robots?

They may dive into every yawn
I foment, to copy the hue of my pleasure,
And see if they can drop the same,
But they won't copy my sleep.

We executed two successful world wars
Before they arrived.
The Squirrel

Whether beautiful or ugly,
The flamingo with its feet trapped
 In a fisherman's net & the squirrel
Running from a wildfire may not hold
Account of that quality,
Where you come from,
Or the race to which you belong.

What I Told the Press

I shall pour for you the rainwater
Gathered in a dent above my crown
& if there's no dent,
You should just go cure your thirst
Somewhere else.
Excuse me, my coffee is catching cold.
My dog is sniffing the neighbor's
Steak in my absence.
I should revisit last night's dream.

The Bougainvillea

I have been sent to look
                At the purple flowers
Of the bougainvillea
                In the city garden &
 Unsee its drying leaves.

I have been sent to forget my dreamt   image
Of the tree before I arrive here,
                Just to wear a refined sight.

I Also Said Nothing against that Grasshopper

1

A grasshopper gnaws a leaf

Of green grass, in the shadow

Of a green tuft of grass.

2

My mourning for a grasshopper

Resembles a lament for the grass

In the sweep of brushfires.

Cradle Crave

Here is clean & green,
Where reign the rains
Of brain drain.

Dead Trees

What is it nature losses:
The dry leaves
Putrid, dissolving into earth,
Diffusing a wet stench
Or the things with axes, secateurs,
And wildfires we take before
Nature surrenders it to us?
I did not call a summit
For the green grass I cut
To thatch my house, last year.
Do not say anything against
Dead trees.

I do not feed from any blood
That I let leak into the soil.

turbulence

world,
excuse me truly.
cream white plumeria,
do not let me go.
this journey
is to birth a return
to the emeralds
& the melting of blades.
you have this dance scalding
the soles of my soul.
the trees i love,
you can harvest from them,
but only when you drool
the right turbulence of love.

The Anthill

The morivivi is quiet.

The anthill inhabited

By a mother-snake & her family

Is also quiet.

I am attending to an assembly

Of galloping solitude.

Bad Animals

The morning shadows of sorghum stalks
Streak across my father's grave.
Still nauseating from last night's
Sleeplessness, I scribble down
On a yellow notepad:
"There's a response, not an urge
To write about the acts of bad animals
& callous people.
But callous people first, I have not yet
Buried a victim of the cruelty of animals"

So When Is the Apocalypse?

The mother-kite spent days plaiting a nest,
Grass leaf after another,
Then came a hand vying for sainthood
And plucked it to the ground.
Now, wingless nestles shriek in the grass,
In mixture of white & grey droppings.

Golden Ladder

For the missing rung
In the golden ladder,
The fault is all mine.
I deserve to stand in the guilty line.
Stop sniffing into my shit for gold!
I am not talking to you,
I am talking to God.

Glass Plate

With this soft skin &   breakable bones,

Can I go around breaking

Other bodies like a glass plate

Raised to   break all visible rocks?

How can I keep away from stains

Like a star?

When should each crack of skin sing

My own pain &

Each pour, my inner colour?

I May Not Apply for a Demigod

       1

I have suspicions about owning a demigod.
What if he shits a lot, wears diapers,
And he is not allowed to clean his own shit.
 I think my god cannot be dirty,
Which points at me & my hands.

2

You see, sometimes, a human god can give me
A morsel, then ask me to vomit it,
A few days later.

3

My god may host envy when I gift
A gourdful of milk to his creator.

       4

What if a demigod gets lost
And I am only entitled to chant
Behind him, his wisdom?

5
Also, a human god can grow his ego
In direct proportion to my adoration,
Until my worship can no longer satisfy him.

6
I crave flowers after the first rains,
Somewhere in April and May.
What if I get tasked with counting the hairs
Around his anus?
And remember this is Poetry Month?
And a blue robin is picking something
From the bell of a plumeria.

7
A human god may be allergic to freedom,
Especially when others have it.
I desire to take a sabbatical all the time,
And I might end up slapping the belly
Of a god, and get into a fist-fight,
Then a dog starts to sleep on the pedestal.

Then we become two men in a fight,
Probably with only the dog watching us.

8

First is the intention of a human god
Wanting to be a god.
Then other people may gather around
Their chosen gods,
Then each one decides to be a god
And no one can worship another,
And I become a god to myself.
And now, I have a new problem.

9

There might come a dogma that says:
'One must lose one's common sense to qualify
As a congregant to a god'
What if I need my common sense
To buy a bottle of milk,
And a god is of a lesser profit
At least to me?

10

My god can decide to be a pet lion.
I cannot enjoy watching goats & fowls
Play around its pedestal.

hail the broken hammer

hail

the taxes you give

to architects of human misery

the bullets they were exchanged

for may return to button up

your shirts

to gong brutal nationhood

in patriotic trees

hail

here you can have

your nationalism

it daydreams of lifeless wars

it hopes for tyranny

i wanted something

like a flower in the sudd

or some misty jungle

hail

you may cast

your ballot paper

now

before a bullet can

hole up the tick

before you can

throw it into a burning

flag

hail

may that season

not ripen

of opulent anger

of domineering

greed

of great men

hitting God's pot of oil

with the hungry wagging

of their tails

of great men

doling out abundances

of human suffering

may the sun break

upon cracking

eggs of fruition.

may the wombs

from light

host bloodless

victories

hail

the thought that planets

reigned upon by the sun(s)

during the day

& moon(s) at night

may experience less

human misery

before levitation

rust-dappled
hammer,
are you
any mightier
than the nails
you drill into
palms,
or the hand
that hurls
your fury?

Debris

Ayena,

When is the storm coming?

I want to be what   remains

Whole when   it dies.

I have prepared the muscle

Of my mind to pick out

Of the hurricane a branch

Of any tree.

stories

hok alam,
stories have no hands
to paint their footprints.
here is my rising tongue,
a chip of your war nails,

screaming in silence
this thirst for a louse's blood
may be cowardice,
and these war cries
songs of the last
dance under the garrulity of
rusting yesterday's moons.
where in sweet sleep do arks
save men from
floods this generous,
floods of wrath whirling
inside men?
where in the tumult of proud
wrath can rains fall?

A Crucible

The cadaver in anatomy lab,
As if warned of hands
That will search him sans his permission,
Stretched arms stiff as iron bars.
The time Fouza fell and broke with her butt
A crucible, was our first shot at bending in the arms,
The morning we forced him to let it go.

Dear Crown

You will not have the moon;
It is so beautiful on your royal house.
You will not have mars now;
It is space shuttle away,
And the air there may drown you.

My wings grow so fast pushing away
The barbed wire,
Pushing away your wants.

Small Mirrors before Mountains

By what measure do I match you,
A woman writhing on a childbed
Like million needles bit you?

My body is wearied by sharks
Of ravenous longing.

Sometimes, I feel ground & reared
By labours my bone sires,

I am tethered by things
That fill me with delight.

My pledge will not let this string
Of honey slide off my tongue
As the bluebell
Grows from blue to ashes.

By what measure do I compare
To you, a man turning in the mirror

Glow for glow?

I untidy my hair
Whenever I intend my thoughts.

But Your Shadow Drowns a Flea

Of kin to the fluttering cobweb
That can be construed for wind's skeleton,
I vaporized from your soothing claw,
Red in my liver.
Do? Savor razorblades slit my liver?
Schmooze pyramids to peg me into earth?

I got spat out to this land,
Old charred bamboos,
Their standing undone,
Were Abuks and Dengs.

Wingless feet teleported my mind
To Rum-e-nyiel & doled there the calmness
Of mist-buttered trees
And the crouching lake of dim tolerance,
Rum-e-nyiel, where noise has no footprints.

Still, your shrapnel words with a wild-dog's hunger
Came hewing the grass leaves of voiceless thoughts,

Only to fall down as strands of cotton,
Besides blue feathers of crested cranes.

I Wrote a Poem

One day, under a deciduous tree,
I wrote a poem.
Each word fell with every yellow
Leaf that touched earth.

A goat ate it while I was answering a call.
'Well, the goat possibly needed it'
But then I remembered the goat only loved
The paper but not the words.
I sat down to craft it, word for leaf
And kept it to myself,
Until now that you are the only person
Reading it.

Is This the Lake?

Dark still water mirror blue feathery clouds,
The wind blows from its vapors into my nostrils
Smell of fresh dampness.
There's a promise of rain far beyond the floodplain
Where the mangrove trees assemble guard, mark
The edges, and vex gale winds.
The green weeds sway mirthfully, their bottoms soaked
In soft dark mud.
Many years ago, cattle-keepers had land disputes &
 Skulls marked its shores before they banished.

A Rap Encore for Hunger

Verse 1

See!
I am not talking about the brains
That canes enticed to run the race,
But rather the pains that made the veins run
The lanes.
The humongous hunger that allows me to tread
With untrammeled gait,
 Ignoring any bait that would let me wait.

Verse 2

My appetite for the heights remains dry
Even when the tides of time try to bite it,
As I stay awake in my sleep.
I don't break the fast first when I break awake
But bake a dreaded bread
That will break the fast so fast.

A Likely Crime in a Rhyme

Lick liquor…stand stupor.

Bite bitter…..spit spittle.

Wage wars….weary worry.

Skip sleep…doze dazed.

Run Rivers…build bridges.

Rip rags….buy bales.

Zap zeal…blemish bliss.

Hunt hunger….bake bread.

The Song of Beams

Bright beams blurred bleak,
& blue-black branded bright.
Deal: decode decadent deception.
Life can lay low leaving living
Lax or languid.

These Songs

These songs, I sing them because
I eschewed some gods.
I chased the god of sellable bliss
And burnt his amulets.
I can now bring crocodile's teeth
& leopard's spots into my odes,
Just for the sake of mischief.
I bring skunks into my songs
Just so you cannot cover your nostrils.
These songs do not be rhyme to your whines.
These songs are eagles;
Their landing cannot be commanded.

There Is Something You Seek.

There's something you are looking for.
It might be what a street kid
Searches for in rotting garbage,
What rain looks for on ice-dressed soil,
What ants search for in empty groundnut pods.

Again, there's something you seek.
It might be what hawks
Look for in the ashes of a burnt savanna,
What ghosts look for in a deserted house.
What dogs look for in a deserted town,
Or what the people look for in harvested fields.

Because You are Just a Poet

You cannot understand clearly
 Our fears here, standing by a wrecked car
In the middle of a large African forest.
You cannot!
These fears running our veins dry.
All the leopards' howls you dub:
Nature's breaking of silence,
The biting cold you call night's soothing
Expiration,
And the darkness you call God's closed eye,
Could be less your horrors.

Mekanika

Jet-black
Greasy hands,
A matching overall,
Smell of engine oil,
Car-tyre shoes, your dark glasses,
And your sun-whacked back
Put my old piece back on the road
And your bread on the plate,
Small town's mechanic.

The Nile's Burdens

The Nile too roars,
 Trying to roll over boulders
 As the thorn trees
Give permanent audience.

Other Mirrors

Once, I said to myself:
"You are the one that is lost.
Crust of rust formed on your face"

I have been looking for mirrors to prove.
I saw it through this one that claims I am half-here,
But the mirrors I dread are the ones that reflect
I never existed.

A Troubadour's Trouble

Heedless hoodlums drumming
Harmful hums numb in a humid hub
And laughing out loud
Can be troubadour's trouble.

Who Told You to Be God?

   1

Why are you arranging in lines
The pieces
Of my broken pot.

I left them on top
Of each other,
In random order.
Don't you have a broken one?

   2

I sing a verse in protest of the colony
Of clogged paths, dry bones, and
              The futility of justice.

 What again is your chorus?

3

On a wet concrete flour,

Tiny black ants

        Stream into a soaked piece

Of brown bread.

They probably do not warrant your royalty.

4

This rough scar on my right ankle

Is from a cut I won when I jumped

Over a young palm tree.

This cannot be yours too.

5

The frogs also have these songs

They never invite anyone

To be their choirmaster.

6

The crested crane you shot dead
Today may never dance in your watch &
In the rain, these trees vow more
To a tempest.

7

The legend of Tung Col talks of deity
Who ate a peanut paste from a hand
Of a young boy, before slipping into a wood.

Now, get your dirty claws out of my ghee!

The Guest

We do not publish on billboards

The tiny bits of snow hanging

On your eyebrows.

Sorry, we do not print images of air.

What you see printing is for one company.

Their oil is sold all over the world.

We do not advertise fumes from cars & factories.

Raining Hope

Solemn child,

Is there a songbird

In the winds

Singing hymns of your rise?

God's silence

Resurrects in thunders,

Yet no thunder has been loud enough

To quake with raining hope

The whole earth,

So, solemn one,

Is there a fire-bathed bolt

Drooling down our breath?

Or am I to replace all waiting

With rivers & trees & rains…?

the tulip

the tulip,
earth's petalled
tongue,
may not be here
to magnify
anyone's flaws
but to shade
its craft.

You Could Have Ceased an Entire Holocaust

1

The three cows returned,

Their udders inflated & their teats sharp.

You could have let the calves suckle to their fill,

Then milk the cows,

But you filled your gourd before releasing

The calves.

The calves you left in the rain, yesterday afternoon.

2

The guerrilla warriors in the Congo

Do not watch for long the ores of gold & coltan.

Sometimes, the ores are underground

& sometimes, they have to watch the sky

For missiles & flying grenades.

3

In North Kivu,

A young boy dives into a thick shrub,

His goat leashed to his hand.

Of course, the bullets missed him.
He probably did not see the rainbow
Above his head.

4
People also mourn in Gaza.
People may also party in Gaza,
Same anywhere God can profit most
In the onions, parsley, and the flowers…

5
God has not registered any grudges
Against unarmed children, women, & men
In Gaza, at least in this poem.

dappled

green & yellow
dappled ore of gold
from wet earth,
wearing half-shine
&
you bluebell, your glee is not yet
ruined by judgment,
nor will the journey of the ore
into glittering necklace
be paused by indifference.

The Churchyard Song

While holding your hands,
I glance at the full moon rising
Behind the mesh of leafless twigs
Of the acacia tree.
It appears like a white ball at end
Of a standing broom.
My fingers feel like the strings of a guitar
  The veins at the back of your hands.

'It is too early for the hoot of the owl'

Your smiles uncage mine as we slow-dance
Between the grass-thatched church & the tree.
The brinded cat that follows us to this yard
  Pulls playfully, with its teeth, the strand of leather
  On my left shoe.

I long for the night to dissolve the aches & loves
  Strung as beads behind us.

May we surrender to that light
Brighter than ourselves & the moon,
 Now detached
From the mesh of leafless twigs.

The Turtle

The boys assemble
Over the wet turtle,
Thrown out of the river
By the fishermen.
The voting has three of the five
Boys claiming ownership.
When it is finished,
They look around for officers
Of the Wild Life Authority.
A whistle blows from a black canoe
Down the river.
There is a big boat coming

The Red Tulips

I bypassed you tending red tulips,
Because I mend broken things
And you are not broken.

The tulips did not ask to be tended,
And the sun above them did not ask
To be applauded.

The Game

The game for me is tricky
-To shoot dead a man,
Then ask another corpse
To join my giggle.

War Republic

We can no longer wage wars
  For lice lost in hair plantations
Nor can we resuscitate flies
Drowned in acidic piss.
We cannot wash shit off their feet
As did Rabbi to his seller,
For the gods of death assailed us,
Even when sacrificial chicken
Made headless dances at our nail-less feet.
The river we wanted to cross towards God
Froze at our knees and that may be
How vultures choked on eyeballs
Reaped from the wars we brew,
That may be how maggots of animosity
  By Darwin's evil-ution thronged vicinity.

Golden Eagle

Perhaps, no one knows
How the sculptor took flight away
From this golden eagle,
Upon this pedestal.

The path I am searching for, lives
In some land I have not seen,
But I know the path exists.

The path leads to where a morsel
Is not unglued from hunger &
And golden eagle is handed back its flight.

Affidavit

Those who got lost are also calling:
'Come, be one of us.
You'll find great company'

But the chirp of the chickadee
In the tamarind trees
Invites me over for a duet.

This Says It Is Love

This says it is love,
Selling me its broken pots
And lands that suck
Litres of dreams from my veins,
& put rotting buds of hemlock
Down my throat.

I am writing odes about drying trees
& broken axes.

A Lament for a Flower

Green breeds of wild pitchers
Nourished by wet roots their breeds
To suck of a blooded bread.
Now, we dance upon our land &
Hear rumbles of despotic belches.
At times, we breathe in republican airs
Thick with aromas of burnt gunpowder.

Lumiére

I see a bright full moon tonight,
But two committees are here:
One is tasked to let me say
That I am seeing something else
& another to convince me
That I am seeing nothing.

Jasmine

This is what I am saying,
I ran away from the claws of darkness.
You can see torn pieces of my shirt
Lighting its mouth.
You should believe it,
Else, I shall forever do.

And this is another thing I want to say,
Renewal is the dialect of all mornings
And you should not forget this new breath
For a wither.
I find it half sad to replace sadness
With nothing.
Here, at the edge of a green plain,
There's a jasmine
Growing from the wet dark soil,
Under a fan palm tree.

But Please, Bless Us

We step on ants.

Some of us cut down trees
To make furniture & this paper.

Some of us start wars
Just in hope to gain peace.

Some feed on the root
Of our own fruition.

Some kill elephants
To take away their tusks.

We walk into destruction
You did not allot to us.

Sometimes, when people we love die,
We light candles under full moons
& sing,

A drop of blood for your angel
To tread upon.

But please, bless us.

Cinematography

1

I find it rare, to get shot in the leg
And still have a flaming cigarette
In one's mouth.

2

Live from memory, I hear my grandfather
Sing of his bull that learnt to swim,
But sometimes sinks from its weightiness.
I'm still learning to let that old slouch
  Of the sad part of my history
  Slip off me as I wake up every second.

3

I'm also here, eyeing a beautiful plain.
I have not found the magnitude
Of gratitude for me waking
Up in the depth of honey,
Washed clean of a drowning.

4

You can say some grabbed with both brows
Their idea of the purpose of life,
And are sworn to never let it go.

5

Perhaps, the sculptures of some gods don't breathe,
See, or hear, even the songs sung to them
With hypnotizing solemnity.
My grandfather's god was a branch of a tamarind tree.
The white ants gnawed at its root in red earth,
As he sacrificed chickens and goats.
One time, I overheard him asking for life.

6

Why are you cutting out the bleeding parts
 Of other people's stories,
When the blood is not coming from you?

7

They are always folded inside me,
In amniotic silence,

The wings I can use to fly towards God.

Ode for a Post-war Period

I did not see any child get shot
While breastfeeding in that war.
I saw people run away
From the city they once danced in,
Some in army fatigues.

In most of our wars,
The discotheques go quiet &
 People actually die.
The television does not catch
 All the destruction
& trauma & trauma & trauma…

The warlords do not say:
'Let the children come to us'
And our dreams do not ask:
'What do forests earn from the inferno
They embrace on large scale?'

To Fruit One's Sight

To love one's butter
In the hot sun.

To adore flowers
One cannot bloom.

To have a bruise at heart
And donate more joy.

To live nobody's death.

To repay any wings
One set on fire.

To dig into the core
Of mystery,
For wordless beauty.

To smile away
From bladed tongues.

To breathe light into words.

To wink at the hiss of morning.

To avoid shitting into a Well assigned
To wash the feet of one's seller.

To wake up at the depth of joy.

To live in one's free soul.

To sip one's honey in the rain.

In My Room

I hear the sound of a flute
From where cows graze,
He may be living in this land.
I hear the songs of the dancers
From the village playground,
Though sometimes, they are faint.
The morning glories flanking
My door are pink.
Last December, the motes from distant
Brushfires covered them.
I had to clean them & return to immerse
In peaceful solitude,
Which I find society rarely grants me.

The Deity of Switches

You see your face changing
To his,
And your nails, they are darker
Than your former,
And your new feet are heavier
Than you can carry.
Your hair is more crinkled.
This mirror is to let you know,
You have achieved your dream;
You wanted your face
To look like his.

The new soul, you can taste it
As it diffuses into you,
And its bitterness captures you,
And you cannot run away.

Look, for this ocean before you,
Welcome to a desert!

This Place

Not everything
You see here is all there is;
This place is not everywhere.
The trees you see here
Are not arranged as you desire
Them, in a land far away,
But my yearning resembles my yearning
& my dreams come ringing bells
Of cryptic autonomy.
The rain is not dying…
They government is not hoarding famine…

Camera

After the war,
I saw three young boys
Run from a photographer
Who aimed his camera
At a setting sun,
I hid from handshakes of warlords;
What if something is in my palm
And can hardly be kept,
Just like our current peace?

Dark Doors

(In Ishaka, on 12th September, 2015)

There is a small house
With a dark door
At the edge of the forest.

I never entered that house.
I saw it first when near it
A young girl was raped
& strangled to death.

There was a crowd
But only the police dog
Sniffed a dark iron door.

There can be other dark doors
I don't want to knock.

Marshall Islands

Invitation Letter

You probably said:
We have chosen you, Marshall Islands.
All our studies favoured you;
Your palm trees, beaches,
Forests & your lives.

We are dropping them here,
Upon your skins.
American bombs fall where America
Deems fit.

Genghis Khan

You saw our land and fell
Into Genghis Khan's sleepy awe.
Marshall Islands,
You are all ours; even your ashes.

The Script

The script is not always clear
As one's skin, & the mirror
Into the future
Is not easily available,
Like a puke of pearl & sunlight.
God never goes to sleep;
Ngundeng said,
People are cows of God.
Did He even gift to Himself
A single slumber?
All, but whatever God
Watches over may be of value.
Perhaps, darkness is not just scared
Of our suspicions.
Where's Abel?
Where are the mammoths I put here?
Why are the trees not the same?
Come here, my children.
Sleep in my arms.
Allow the worries

On your mind to dream.

Mmap New African Poets Series

If you have enjoyed *Who Told You To Be God*, consider these other fine books in the Mmap New African Poets Series from *Mwanaka Media and Publishing:*

I Threw a Star in a Wine Glass by Fethi Sassi
Best New African Poets 2017 Anthology by Tendai R Mwanaka and Daniel Da Purificacao
Logbook Written by a Drifter by Tendai Rinos Mwanaka
Mad Bob Republic: Bloodlines, Bile and a Crying Child by Tendai Rinos Mwanaka
Zimbolicious Poetry Vol 1 by Tendai R Mwanaka and Edward Dzonze
Zimbolicious Poetry Vol 2 by Tendai R Mwanaka and Edward Dzonze
Zimbolicious: An Anthology of Zimbabwean Literature and Arts, Vol 3 by Tendai Mwanaka
Under The Steel Yoke by Jabulani Mzinyathi
Fly in a Beehive by Thato Tshukudu
Bounding for Light by Richard Mbuthia
Sentiments by Jackson Matimba
Best New African Poets 2018 Anthology by Tendai R Mwanaka and Nsah Mala

Words That Matter by Gerry Sikazwe

The Ungendered by Delia Watterson

Ghetto Symphony by Mandla Mavolwane

Sky for a Foreign Bird by Fethi Sassi

A Portrait of Defiance by Tendai Rinos Mwanaka

Zimbolicious: An Anthology of Zimbabwean Literature and Arts, Vol 4 by Tendai Mwanaka and Jabulani Mzinyathi

When Escape Becomes the only Lover by Tendai R Mwanaka

ويَسهَرُ اللَّيلُ عَلَى شَفَتي...وَالغَمَام by Fethi Sassi

A Letter to the President by Mbizo Chirasha

This is not a poem by Richard Inya

Pressed flowers by John Eppel

Righteous Indignation by Jabulani Mzinyathi:

Blooming Cactus by Mikateko Mbambo

Rhythm of Life by Olivia Ngozi Osouha

Travellers Gather Dust and Lust by Gabriel Awuah Mainoo

Chitungwiza Mushamukuru: An Anthology from Zimbabwe's Biggest Ghetto Town by Tendai Rinos Mwanaka

Zimbolicious: An Anthology of Zimbabwean Literature and Arts, Vol 5 by Tendai Mwanaka

Because Sadness is Beautiful? by Tanaka Chidora

Of Fresh Bloom and Smoke by Abigail George

Shades of Black by Edward Dzonze

Best New African Poets 2020 Anthology by Tendai Rinos Mwanaka, Lorna Telma Zita and Balddine Moussa

This Body is an Empty Vessel by Beaton Galafa

Between Places by Tendai Rinos Mwanaka

Best New African Poets 2021 Anthology by Tendai Rinos Mwanaka, Lorna Telma Zita and Balddine Moussa

Zimbolicious: An Anthology of Zimbabwean Literature and Arts, Vol 6 by Tendai Mwanaka and Chenjerai Mhondera

A Matter of Inclusion by Chad Norman

Keeping the Sun Secret by Mariel Awendit

سِجلٌ مَكتُوبٌ لتَائِهِ by Tendai Rinos Mwanaka

Ghetto Blues by Tendai Rinos Mwanaka

Zimbolicious: An Anthology of Zimbabwean Literature and Arts, Vol 7 by Tendai Rinos Mwanaka and Tanaka Chidora

Best New African Poets 2022 Anthology by Tendai Rinos Mwanaka and Helder Simbad

Dark Lines of History by Sithembele Isaac Xhegwana

a sky is falling by Nica Cornell

Death of a Statue by Samuel Chuma

Along the way by Jabulani Mzinyathi

Strides of Hope by Tawanda Chigavazira

Young Galaxies by Abigail George

Coming of Age by Gift Sakirai

Mother's Kitchen and Other Places by Antreka. M. Tladi

Best New African Poets 2023 Anthology by Tendai Rinos Mwanaka, Helder Simbad and Gerald Mpesse

Zimbolicious Anthology Vol 8 by Tendai Rinos Mwanaka and Mathew T Chikono

Broken Maps by Riak Marial Riak

Formless by Raïs Neza Boneza

Of poets, gods, ghosts. Irritants and storytellers by Tendai Rinos Mwanaka

Ethiopian Aliens by Clersidia Nzorozwa

In The Inferno by Jabulani Mzinyathi

Soon to be released

www.ingramcontent.com/pod-product-compliance
Lightning Source LLC
Chambersburg PA
CBHW070848160426
43192CB00012B/2361